GENERAL FEATURES

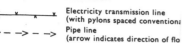 Electricity transmission line
(with pylons spaced convention: r)

  Pipe line
(arrow indicates direction of flo

  Quarry

  Open pit

  Wood

Orchard

Park or ornamental grounds

  Bracken, heath and rough grassland

  Dunes

+ Graticule intersection at 5′ intervals

△ Triangulation pillar

☼ Windmill (in use)

♀ Windmill (disused)

♈ Wind pump

▲ Youth hostel

RELIEF

—— 76 —— Contour values are given to the nearest metre. The vertical interval is, however, 50 feet

·44 Heights are to the nearest metre above mean sea level.

BOUNDARIES

- + — + — + National

-o- -o- -o- -o- London Borough
National Park

—·—·—·— County or
Metropolitan County

············· Civil Parish or
equivalent

NT
} National Trust { always open

NT { opening restricted

ABBREVIATIONS

· Post office

·H Public house

·H Club house

·MP Mile post

·MS Mile stone

TH Town hall, Guildhall or equivalent

PC Public convenience (in rural areas)

.T
.A } Telephone call box {
.R

PO
AA
RAC

ANTIQUITIES

·LLA Roman

·mulus Non-Roman

+ Site of antiquity

⚔ 1066 Battlefield (with date)

© Crown copyright 1974

Maps are fascinating things, and once we have learned to read them they can supply us with much interesting — as well as useful — information.

Everyone needs to read maps at some time, and this book shows how easily they can be understood.

Maps

by NANCY SCOTT
with illustrations by RONALD LAMPITT

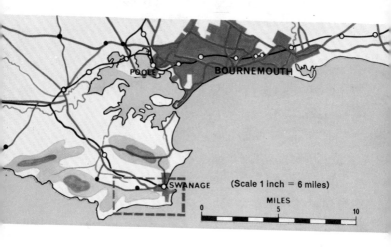

POOLE

BOURNEMOUTH

SWANAGE   (Scale 1 inch = 6 miles)

MILES

0   5   10

Ladybird Books Loughborough

The Globe

Thousands of years ago, man believed that the world was flat and surrounded by sea, so he drew his maps on flat sheets of parchment, papyrus or baked clay tablets.

We now know that the world is round and spins on its axis, and we can therefore depict the whole of the world on a globe, dividing it into sections with accurately drawn lines which a navigator on land, sea or in the air can use to guide him from one place to another.

The picture shows you the position of the two poles. The half-circles drawn from pole to pole are called lines of *longitude*, and each one is numbered. One line of longitude passes through Greenwich, near London, and is numbered 0°. The other lines of longitude are numbered east and west of Greenwich until they meet on the opposite side of the globe at 180 degrees (180°).

Midway between the two poles a line is drawn *round* the globe. This is called the Equator and is also numbered 0°. The other lines similar to it are called lines of *latitude* and are numbered north and south from the Equator.

By using these lines and reference numbers we can give the position on the globe of any place in the world. London is *latitude* 51° 30′N. *longitude* 00° 05′W.

A globe

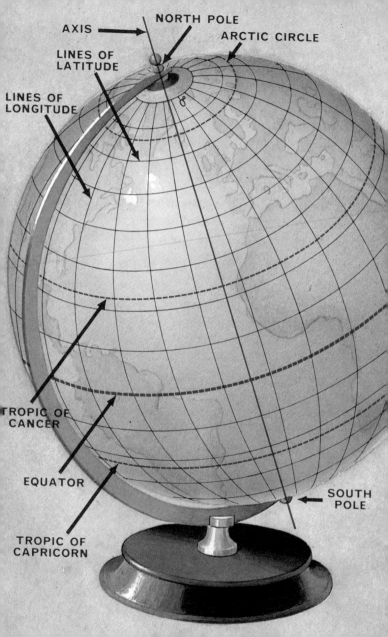

The Problem of Map-Making

Early explorers made full use of the globe in navigating their ships. The oldest surviving globe is one made in the year of Columbus' first voyage to America, but of course it has no mention of America on it. The maker of this globe covered a ball-shape with strips of parchment, and on this he drew and coloured the world as it was then known.

Famous sea-captains, such as Sir Walter Raleigh, Magellan and Drake always used a pair of globes when plotting their course. One globe showed the stars in the heavens, the other the earth.

If you tried to cut open a globe from north to south pole and lay it flat on the table, you would find that the lines of longitude go up and down the map, and the lines of latitude across it. But in trying to make your map lie flat you would discover that the top and bottom would have to be stretched out and this would alter the shapes and sizes of the countries, and the lines of latitude and longitude also.

All flat maps therefore have to be distorted, as you can see in the picture. It is only on the round surface of a globe that all the lands and seas can be shown accurately.

The picture shows you how the distortion increases in the extreme northern and southern regions, the map only appearing accurate at the Equator.

Portion of a globe and a map showing distortion on map of land and sea areas

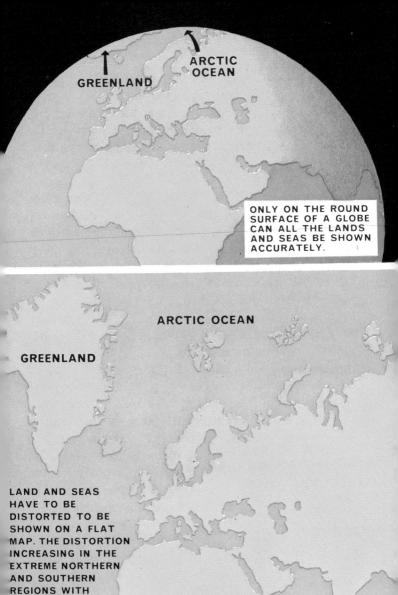

GREENLAND

ARCTIC OCEAN

ONLY ON THE ROUND
SURFACE OF A GLOBE
CAN ALL THE LANDS
AND SEAS BE SHOWN
ACCURATELY.

ARCTIC OCEAN

GREENLAND

LAND AND SEAS
HAVE TO BE
DISTORTED TO BE
SHOWN ON A FLAT
MAP. THE DISTORTION
INCREASING IN THE
EXTREME NORTHERN
AND SOUTHERN
REGIONS WITH
ACCURACY ONLY AT
THE EQUATOR.

The Atlas

A distorted map is, of course, useless for navigation by sea or land. Sailors found that they failed to get to their destination when they drew a straight line on their maps or charts and tried to sail on that course. The stretching had caused the true compass direction to be altered.

A man named Geradus Mercator solved the problem. He divided the globe into twelve gores which, when spread out, lay flat and yet still left the compass directions as straight lines. When the twelve gores were fitted together they once more made a perfect globe-shape. All ships and aircraft still use charts and maps drawn by Mercator's method.

Very early maps had to be copied by hand, but when printing was invented maps of all shapes and sizes appeared in great numbers. Because separate sheets of assorted sizes were troublesome to handle, a publisher named Ortelius tried printing the maps on sheets all the same size and binding them together as a book. This was a great success, but his book was not given the name by which we now call such a collection of maps. A few years later Mercator produced a new collection of maps and called it an *Atlas*. Atlas was the name of a legendary Greek hero who was said to hold up the heavens on his shoulders.

Now, a collection of maps bound like a book is always called an atlas, even in some other languages.

How Mercator divided the globe into twelve gores

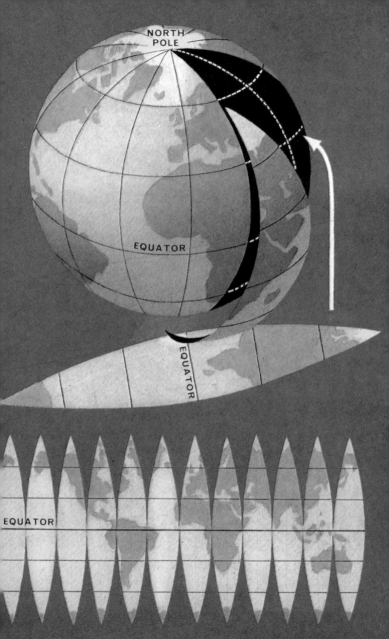

NORTH
POLE

EQUATOR

EQUATOR

EQUATOR

Scale

Every map is drawn to a scale, whether a map of the world or a map of a particular local area. The scale of a map enables us to measure the exact distances between any places marked on it. It does not matter whether the map is drawn to Imperial or Metric scale for these purposes.

In the top illustration opposite is a section of the South Coast from a map on the scale of 1-inch to a mile. This means that two places shown as 1 inch apart are actually about one mile apart.

This map shows the town of Swanage in some detail. But look what happens in the same size space when you draw a map on a scale of six miles to an inch. Now Swanage covers a much smaller area, and a great deal more of the surrounding coastal area has been included. Poole Harbour is shown, and beyond that the big coastal town of Bournemouth.

The scale in the map at the bottom is even smaller, and now the same space includes many towns on the South Coast, but very little localised detail.

Every large scale map carries a scale line, usually at the foot of the map. This is for measuring distances on the map. The first section is subdivided, so that any part of a mile can be measured with accuracy.

Different scales of maps

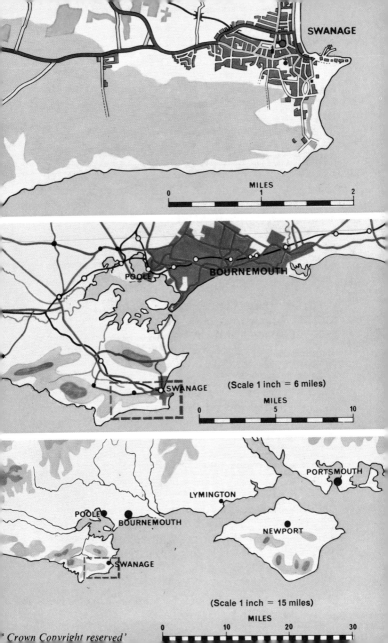

SWANAGE

0 MILES 1 2

POOLE BOURNEMOUTH

SWANAGE (Scale 1 inch = 6 miles)

0 MILES 5 10

PORTSMOUTH

LYMINGTON

POOLE BOURNEMOUTH

NEWPORT

SWANAGE

(Scale 1 inch = 15 miles)

0 MILES 10 20 30

Ordnance Survey Maps

The main maps we use nowadays are published by the British Ordnance Survey Department. This Government department was set up in 1791 to prepare maps of Britain in a uniform manner. The country was developing rapidly, and accurate maps were needed for work on canals, railways, new roads, drainage schemes and industrial development.

To prepare these maps, the land had to be thoroughly surveyed and measured, and a system worked out whereby every detail could be recorded accurately on paper, and yet take up the least possible space. Special signs, symbols and colouring were therefore used, and these signs and symbols, known as *conventional mapping signs*, are explained on every complete map.

The first maps the department published were on the scale of 1-inch to a mile. This was the most popular scale in general use, but it has now been replaced by the slightly larger scale of 1:50 000 (approximately $1\frac{1}{4}''$ to the mile).

Once you have become familiar with the various symbols and devices used in these Ordnance Survey maps, you can pick up a map of any part of the country and read it as you would the page of a book. Look at the scene at the top of the picture opposite; now look at this same scene reproduced as a section of a map below.

Without any further explanation of signs and symbols you can easily identify the main features of the scene as they are shown on the map. Some of the symbols may mystify you for a while, but these are explained in more detail later in the book.

How a map indicates the landscape

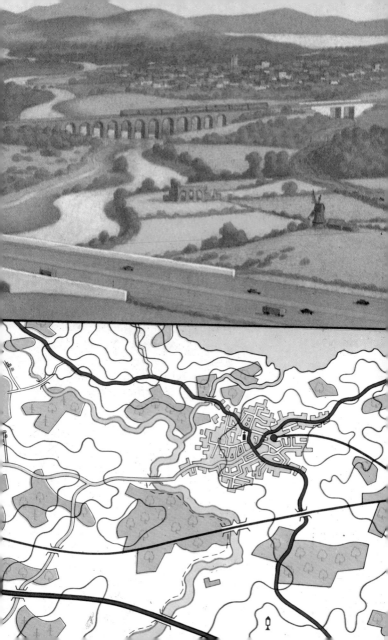

Setting Your Map

Every map is printed with the north at the top of the sheet, and to read and follow a map correctly in unknown country, a compass must be used.

In the right hand margin of every Ordnance Survey map are two arrows. One points *true north*, the other to the *magnetic north* which is the direction in which a compass needle points. The angle between the two arrows is known as the magnetic variation, and this has to be taken into account when navigating by sea and air.

To set your map, place your compass on it and wait for the needle to point north. Now keep the compass steady, and move the map round until the top of the map points towards the north as indicated by compass needle.

If you have no compass handy, you can still set your map accurately by using your watch. Point the hour hand towards the sun, or where you know the sun

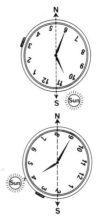

would be at that time of day. Imagine a line joining the centre of the watch face to the figure 12, and another one halfway between this line and the hour hand. This second imaginary line would point due south; so north will be exactly opposite. Don't forget to make allowance for 'Summer Time', if it is in operation. This means taking away one hour from the time recorded by your watch, so if the hour is four o'clock you point the numeral three towards the sun.

Setting a map with a compass

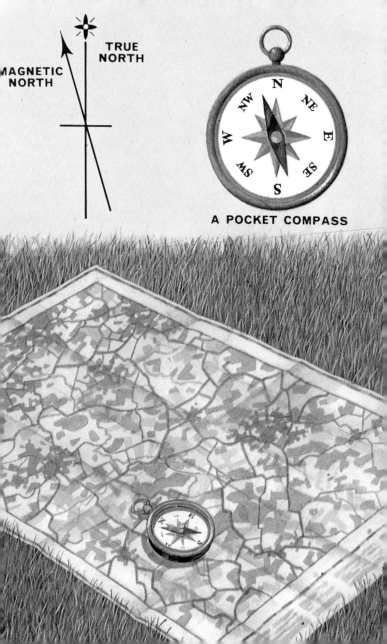

TRUE
NORTH

MAGNETIC
NORTH

A POCKET COMPASS

The Grid System

When you look for a place on a map or globe, you use the lines of longitude and latitude as your guides, but it is not possible to use these reference lines on maps drawn to a larger scale. Instead grid lines are used, a system of vertical and horizontal lines which divide the map into squares.

The Ordnance Survey 1:50 000 maps have lines spaced one kilometre apart and numbered 1 to 100. On the 1:250 000 ($\frac{1}{4}$-inch) maps they are ten kilometres apart and numbered 1 to 10. These grid lines are based on a National Grid system in which the whole area of the British Isles is divided into squares with 100 kilometre sides and with a two letter reference for each square.

By using the grid line numbers we can give a location for any place on a map. The method used is to quote the number of the line to the west of the point and then the number of the line to the south. The reference for Fambridge Station would be 8.9 but you can give its position more accurately if you imagine that each side of the square is divided into tenths. You can see that Fambridge Station is six tenths east of line 8 and seven tenths north of line 9. So we have the reference 86/97 which is written 8697. The first set of figures—86 are called the 'Eastings' and the second set—97 the 'Northings'.

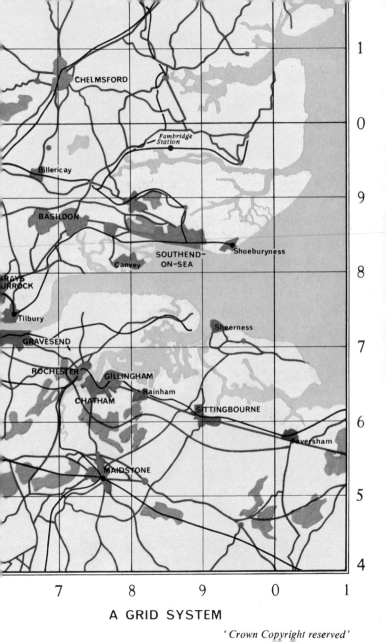

A GRID SYSTEM

Contours

One of the main difficulties that map-makers had to meet was how to show the various land forms—mountains, valleys, plains etc. In Anglo-Saxon times, and for many centuries after, hills and mountains were represented by drawing them in profile, just as you might see them from a distance.

However, this was unsatisfactory, as no scale of height could be shown, and the little 'pictures' blotted out large areas on the maps.

The first two methods used on Ordnance Survey maps were hachuring and hill shading, and both used shading lines. You will find this method on early-printed maps and on certain modern maps where land-forms are more important than detail.

The modern method of showing land relief is by means of *contours*. Contours are lines joining points of the same height. On a 1:50 000 map the contours are drawn to represent 50-foot (15.24 metre) intervals, but the contour values are given to the nearest metre. The lower picture shows you how the presence and height of a hill is depicted in contour lines on a map. On some maps the relief is made still clearer by 'layering', that is the spaces between the contours are shaded in colour-tints of green or brown. The closer the contour lines are to each other, the steeper the hill or mountainside will be, and vertical coastal cliffs are indicated by running one contour into another. The lines also tell you where plains, valleys, escarpments, slopes, spurs, ridges, brows and summits occur.

How contour lines indicate a hill

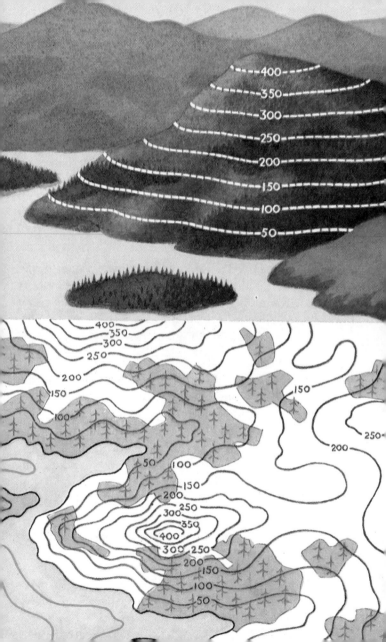

Gradients

Contour lines tell us the height and the situation of hills and mountains. But a climber, a hiker, or a road tourist needs to know whether the slope is gentle or steep. This slope is called the *gradient*, and some gradients are too steep for ordinary vehicles.

When travelling along a road, you have perhaps seen a road sign saying, '1 in 7'. Then immediately afterwards have found yourself going down a particularly steep hill where skilful driving has been needed. Gradients of more than 1 in 7 are shown on all Ordnance Survey maps.

The gradient of a slope between two points is calculated by dividing the rise between the two points by the horizontal distance between them. So, if the rise is 50 metres, and the horizontal distance is 500 metres, that is $\frac{50}{500}$ metres $= \frac{1}{10}$ which is expressed as 1 in 10.

Some special gradients of interest are:

1 in 50 — suitable for road transport, but not considered economically suitable for rail transport.

1 in 15 — Too steep for a cyclist. He should walk if the hill is a long one.

1 in 7 — Steep. A good car and good driving needed.

1 in 5 — Very steep. Cars need to change into low gear.

1 in 3 — Too steep for ordinary vehicles. A steep climb or scramble for walkers.

1 in 1 — Appears almost vertical at first sight.

Examples of gradients

1 in 50

1 in 15

1 in 7

1 in 5

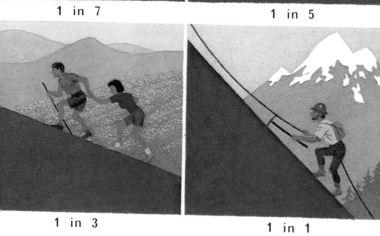

1 in 3

1 in 1

Roads, Railways, Rivers and Canals

You will find that any Ordnance Survey map is criss--
crossed with black, red, brown, yellow and blue lines.
These indicate railways, roads, rivers and canals.

In the top illustration opposite, four grades of road
are shown, the widest being a motorway, built for motor
traffic only, and along which you cannot walk, cycle or
ride a horse. You cannot cross it except by a fly-over
bridge or a pedestrian bridge or tunnel. Roads join a
motorway only at very widely spaced junctions, and
there are no cross-roads.

Motorways are shown in blue. Other major roads are
shown in red, with dual carriageways having thicker
black outlines than single carriageways. Of the roads
shown, the yellow one indicates the narrowest.

Railways are shown by thick black lines, a broken
line indicating a single track. Stations are shown by a
red spot on the line. Where the railway enters a tunnel,
the line is broken into two lines of fine dots.

Rivers and canals are shown by pale blue lines. The
rivers wind about, but the canals, being man-made,
take a straight course. The black V's on the canals show
the position of lock gates.

Notice that in the top picture the 'A' road goes *over*
the motorway so the line of the road is continued;
similarly in pictures 3 and 4 the 'A' road goes over the
river and canal. But in picture 2 the 'A' road goes *under*
the railway line, so the line of the road is broken, while
the railway line is continued.

Some map symbols

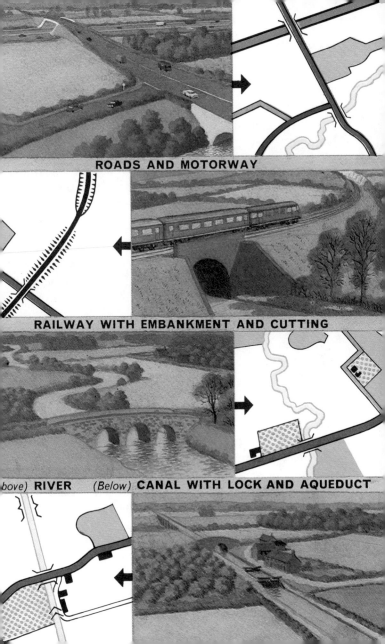

ROADS AND MOTORWAY

RAILWAY WITH EMBANKMENT AND CUTTING

(Above) **RIVER** *(Below)* **CANAL WITH LOCK AND AQUEDUCT**

Symbols

You probably noticed, in the last picture, how the large areas of trees were depicted on the map. The green-coloured patches are woodlands, the white patches are orchards, and the small solid-black patches depict buildings.

The picture opposite shows how a solid mass of buildings is indicated on a map. The larger the village or town, the bigger the shaded grey area will be on the map.

If there is a Post Office in the village it will be identified on the map by the letter P; and a Youth Hostel by the letter Y or a red triangle. A Post Office Telephone Call Box is shown by the letter T, an A.A. Call Box by A, and an R.A.C. Box by R.

An area shaded green on a map, with the letters N.T. printed on it, indicates that it is National Trust land. If the symbol 'N.T.' is printed in red, then the area is always open. But if it is printed in blue, then access to it is restricted.

You can even pick out on many maps where wireless and television masts are sited, the symbol being a miniature mast. Windmills are also shown by a miniature drawing, complete with sails if the windmill is still in use, but without sails if the mill is disused.

A map including a coastline will show the position of the lighthouses and any lightships out at sea—again by miniature drawings.

More map symbols

CHURCH WITH SPIRE

CHURCH WITH TOWER

CHURCH WITHOUT
SPIRE OR TOWER

POST OFFICE

P

Inn

Antiquities

Many other interesting details are shown on a large scale map, and can be read by those who know the conventional mapping signs.

For instance, you can tell if the land you are going to cross will be marshy, rough pasture or parkland, or whether you have to skirt round a quarry, an open pit, a lake or a reservoir. You can also read much of Britain's history by the symbols.

Perhaps you would like to visit some prehistoric remains to see how our early ancestors lived. They built their villages on high ground and surrounded them by earth and stone ramparts; they buried their dead in stone-built chambers and covered the area with earth mounds. These sites are shown on the map either by the name of the site or by such signs as those shown at the top of the illustration.

A castle is also shown either by its name, the word 'Castle' as shown in the illustration, or sometimes by a small symbol.

Many historic battles were fought in this country. The sign of the crossed swords shows you the district, sometimes even the exact fields where these took place.

The Romans occupied our island for some 400 years, and remains of their occupation are to be found all over the country. A Roman villa is marked 'VILLA'. You will also find their fortified camps, their towns, and their straight roads clearly marked.

Symbols for antiquities

PREHISTORIC BURIAL MOUNDS

Long Barrow ✵

Tumuli ✵ ✵

Castle
*LATER THAN
A D 420)*

VILLA

REMAINS OF ROMAN VILLA
(A D 43 to A D 420)

Road Maps

People who have to travel by road on business need maps which show routes clearly. They are not interested in the surrounding countryside or in historic sites, but they *are* interested in the type of road they must travel on: whether it is a straight, wide road which will allow them to travel quickly, or whether it is narrow and winds through villages and towns, thereby adding hours to their travelling time. Special road maps are printed for such people.

Every recognised road in this country has a number. The motorways are numbered M.1 upwards, and the next major roads are prefixed with the letter A. Then come the B roads, linking up with the A roads, and finally the 'other roads' which twist and turn between the larger ones.

Signposts at important cross-roads, and in towns, show the reference numbers as well as place names. A motorist, knowing from his map the number of the road on which he must travel, can read this number easily and quickly on the signpost. A glance at his map also shows him whether the road will take him through a built-up area, or if there is another road he can take to avoid it.

Many towns and cities have by-pass roads. These are major roads built to go round, to by-pass, the congested, heavily built-up town centres. Such by-passes are always clearly marked on maps.

Section of a road map with road numbers

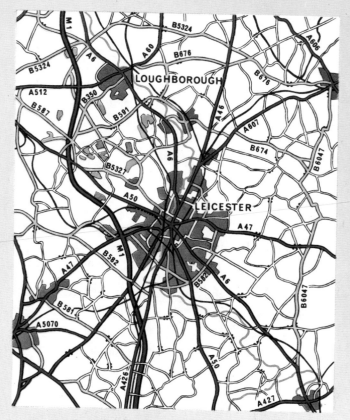

A ROAD MAP with road numbers

MOTORWAY	 **BUILT-UP AREA**
TRUNK or 'A' ROAD	**RIVER and LAKE**
'B' ROAD	**WOOD**
OTHER ROADS	**RAILWAY**

Town Maps

Large scale maps of 50 inches and 25 inches to the mile (1:1250 and 1:2500) are published by the Ordnance Survey Department. These plans are used in local government work, and for all land dealings, because they show every house, road, path, boundary, field, waste land, park and odd patch of land; in fact every single detail of the city, town or village. The various areas of land are given serial numbers and the size of each is shown in acres.

The next size the department does is the '6-inch plan' which shows the same details as the '25-inch plan', but without the serial numbers and sizes of land involved.

A town map published for the convenience of the residents or visitors would be based on the '6-inch plan', and as you can see in our picture, would show where all the most important buildings and features of the town are sited, as well as all the roads.

Some town maps number each feature instead of naming them. In this case you would have to refer to the key at the bottom of the map to find your destination.

The street names, and places of importance, which appear on the map, would also be listed in a key with a grid reference. For instance the Fire Station would be B8.

A typical town map

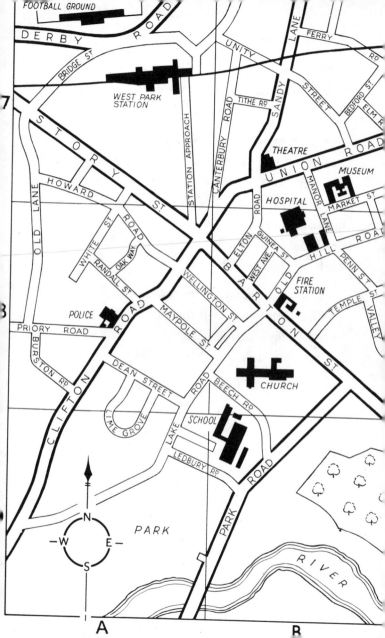

Rural Maps

The details and information given on a rural map will be very different from the information given on a town map.

A town map deals mainly with streets and buildings, but a rural map must show not only the buildings, such as the farms, local school, church, cottages and so on, but also the contours of the land, any quarries, pits, marshes, rough land, woods, ponds, lakes, and all other details which may affect any land deals or development of the area.

Parish and county boundaries are also shown on smaller scale maps, but are difficult to pick out and follow. However, on a large-scale rural map, the boundaries can be clearly seen.

It is also possible on these rural maps to show the type of tree growing in a wooded area. Such details are necessary to the work of the Forestry Commission, who are responsible for the planting and control of large areas of woodland and forest land in this country.

Land drainage schemes can be given preliminary consideration with the aid of this type of map, as it shows the course of any river and the position of marshy or water-logged land.

A rural map

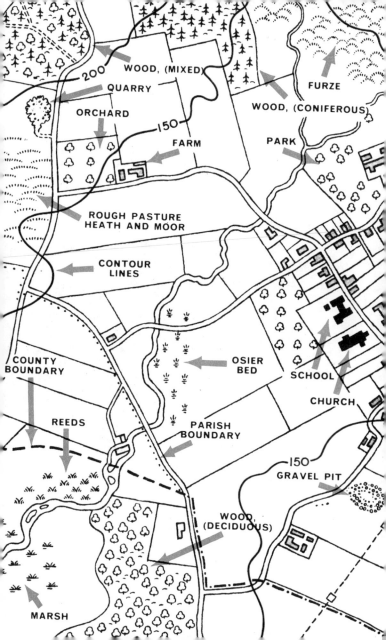

200

WOOD, (MIXED)

QUARRY

ORCHARD

150

FARM

FURZE

WOOD, (CONIFEROUS)

PARK

ROUGH PASTURE
HEATH AND MOOR

CONTOUR
LINES

COUNTY
BOUNDARY

REEDS

OSIER
BED

SCHOOL

CHURCH

PARISH
BOUNDARY

150

GRAVEL PIT

WOOD,
(DECIDUOUS)

MARSH

Physical Maps

Open the first few pages of any atlas and you will find a physical map. This, again, gives special information required by people following certain trades and professions.

The pilot of a plane must know where, and how high, the mountains are, and where the plains are sited, because aerodromes are built on the plains. Ship and submarine captains must know the depth of the sea at various points.

Just as there are mountains, hills, valleys and plains on land, so there are beneath the sea. This means that the sea varies in depth. The height of land is measured in feet or metres *above* sea level, and the depth of sea is measured in feet or metres *below* sea level. A sailor will express the depth of the sea in fathoms. 1 fathom = 6 feet or 1.83 metres.

Notice how much of the colouring of this physical map is sheer common sense. The deeper the sea or ocean, the darker the blue used on the map. The higher the mountain the more likely it is that it will be covered in snow all the year round: so the highest peaks are coloured white. A plain is usually grass-covered, so it is coloured green.

Of course on a physical map showing the whole of the world on one page, you will not get these points so clearly illustrated, but they will be obvious on a larger scale physical map.

Land and sea on a physical map

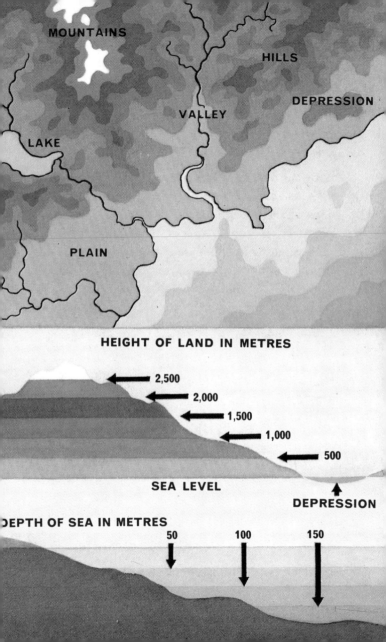

Geology, Population, Rainfall and Land Use Maps

Each of the four small maps opposite gives us further specialised information about our country, and each one can be understood by first studying the small key in its top right-hand corner.

Britain has been in existence on the Earth for many ages, and over these ages the land formation has changed considerably. Mountains have been washed away; plains have become valleys, and valleys inlets of the sea—resulting in different layers of rock being laid bare in many different places. From these layers of rock we can tell the age and the geological history of any part of the country.

From the population map you can pick out the areas of Britain with the most, and the least, number of people living in them per square mile. The annual rainfall map shows you the areas of Britain which have the least amount of rain per year, and the areas with the most. Notice that the highest rainfall is on the western side of the country, particularly where the mountains are sited.

The land use map gives an idea of the main uses to which our land is put. Coal is mined where the black patches are shown. The mixed shading shows you where a variety of grain crops can be grown with satisfactory results in any one area.

Other useful maps

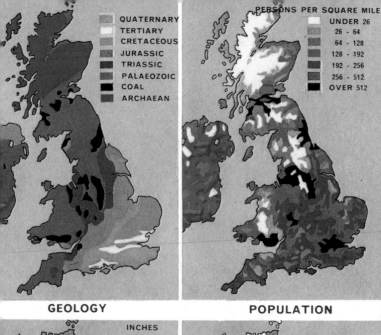

GEOLOGY

QUATERNARY
TERTIARY
CRETACEOUS
JURASSIC
TRIASSIC
PALAEOZOIC
COAL
ARCHAEAN

POPULATION

PERSONS PER SQUARE MILE
UNDER 26
26 - 64
64 - 128
128 - 192
192 - 256
256 - 512
OVER 512

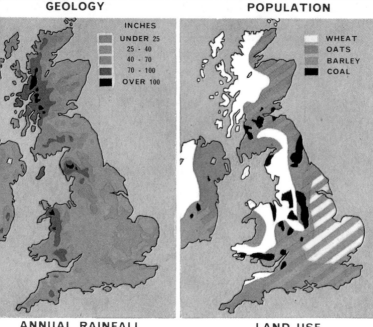

ANNUAL RAINFALL

INCHES
UNDER 25
25 - 40
40 - 70
70 - 100
OVER 100

LAND USE

WHEAT
OATS
BARLEY
COAL

Weather Maps

We all take an interest in the weather, but to some people advance knowledge of weather conditions is essential. The airman, seaman and farmer all need to have this important information.

Like all sciences, meteorology has its own signs and symbols. The wavy lines and curves are *isobars*, and join places where the air pressure is the same. This pressure is the weight of air pressing on every square inch of surface at any one place. Recall to mind the contour lines on a land map, and that by looking at them you could imagine the shapes of the hills and valleys. In the same way isobars represent the 'hollows' and 'humps' in the air above the earth.

The closeness of the isobars also tells us the speed of the wind. The closer the isobars the stronger the wind force. The wind force symbols show the direction of the wind, the 'feathers' on the arrows indicate the speed. A 'full feather' indicates 10 knots, a 'half feather' 5 knots. A knot is a nautical mile (6,080 ft.) per hour. The amount of black in the circles indicates the proportion of cloud cover. When two fronts merge into one another it is called an *occlusion*. Notice the symbol for a warm front and the one for a cold front. Now look again at the one for an occlusion.

LOW means an area of low pressure, a depression, usually rainy.

HIGH means a high pressure area bringing good weather.

Every country collects its own weather observations and exchanges information by radio with other countries.

The symbols on a weather map

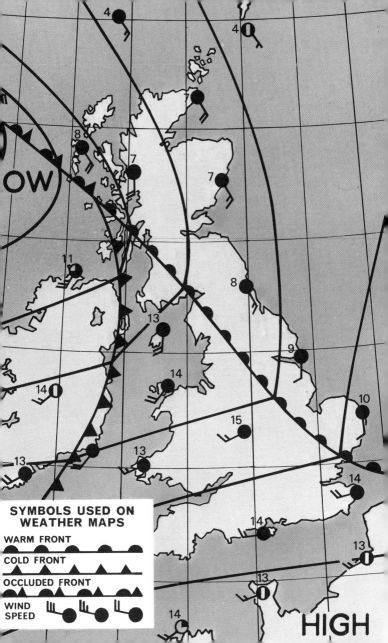

SYMBOLS USED ON
WEATHER MAPS

WARM FRONT

COLD FRONT

OCCLUDED FRONT

WIND
SPEED

LOW

HIGH

Aerial Photography

During this century, the invention of aerial photography has added a new and wonderful excitement to maps and map making. Air survey is helping to complete the mapping of the world in a way undreamed of even fifty years ago. Difficult country such as the Antarctic, deserts, jungles and mountainous regions can now be photographed from the air, and details of whole new areas recorded on maps. Such records have led to the discovery of new deposits of oil, iron ore and other minerals, and have helped in the planning of roads, railways and reservoirs.

Even the early history of a country can be revealed. One of the remarkable things about an aerial photograph is that it can show up detail on the land when hardly a trace of such detail can be seen by people on the ground. In this way the buried remains of ancient settlements and burial chambers have been traced.

Aerial photographs are taken so that they overlap one another. Pairs of photographs are then placed in a *stereoscope*, and this makes objects on the ground—churches, houses, trees, hills—appear to stand out in three dimensions.

For map-making purposes, a stereoscope is built into a special machine which magnifies the scene many times, and from the three-dimensional landscape then seen, a fully-contoured and detailed map can be drawn to any given scale.

The delicate and intricate mechanisms now being sent into Space are providing us with astounding pictures of worlds yet to be mapped and explored.

(top) Aerial photography (bottom) Space photography

Admiralty Charts

The maps used by sailors are called charts, and a ship will carry a great many charts. The small-scale ones show a whole ocean; these are used to plot the voyage and mark the ship's position each day. Large-scale charts show the approaches to ports and are used to navigate through shallower coastal waters.

The physical map showed you that the depth of the ocean varies. A ship's navigator has to know the actual depth of the water, that is the reason for the numerous figures dotted all over an Admiralty Chart. Each of these figures represents the depth in fathoms.

The British Admiralty ships find these depths by using an instrument called an 'echo-sounder'. This works on the fact that a noise made just below the surface of the water travels to the sea bed and the echo travels back again to the surface. The time it takes depends on the depth of the water. By measuring this time, the echo-sounder records the depth. From these records underwater contours are drawn.

The only colours on a sea chart are the grey of land areas, blue tints showing underwater contours, and spots of purple to highlight special aids to navigation such as lighthouses.

Every chart carries a large circle, marked in degrees, showing true and magnetic north, together with the scale and the date of the chart.

An Admiralty chart and some of the things it indicates

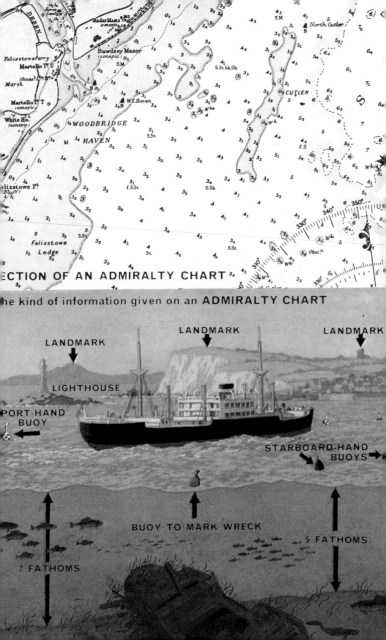

ECTION OF AN ADMIRALTY CHART

The kind of information given on an **ADMIRALTY CHART**

LANDMARK

LANDMARK

LANDMARK

LIGHTHOUSE

PORT-HAND
BUOY

STARBOARD-HAND
BUOYS

BUOY TO MARK WRECK

5 FATHOMS

7 FATHOMS

Navigation at Sea

In the past, seamen found their way at sea by the sun and stars, and these are still used as a sure check today. Because the sun rises in the east and sets in the west, a rough idea of one's position can be worked out if the time of year and time of day are taken into account.

The same principle applies to finding one's way by the stars. You remember that early navigators used a globe of the stars and another of the earth. At night you can always check the direction in which you are moving by first finding the Pole star. In the Northern Hemisphere, the Pole star gives true north within two degrees, and can be picked out by the 'pointers' of the constellation, or group of stars, known as the Plough.

Larger ships now use a *gyrocompass* in conjunction with their charts and other instruments of navigation. A gyrocompass is mounted on gimbals which allow it to stay level when the ship heels over, pitches or rolls. It is kept spinning rapidly by an electric motor, and will point *due north* instead of *magnetic north* once it is set and adjusted. Information from the gyrocompass is then fed automatically to many other parts of the ship, such as the autopilot and radar installation.

Another essential instrument used at sea is the

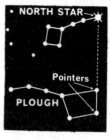

chronometer, a finely-balanced clock which keeps Greenwich time within a fraction of a second a day. An ordinary clock may vary its time with the change in sailing and weather conditions, but not a chronometer. By knowing the exact time, plus the latitude, a sailor can work out the longitude and so his exact position at sea.

A ship's gyrocompass

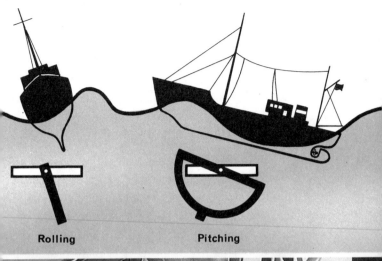

Rolling   **Pitching**

Triangulations

The surveyor has many scientific instruments to help him with his map-making, but he still bases his measuring procedure on the same principle as the early map-makers. Like them, he uses the simplest and yet the most accurate method, known as triangulation.

First a base-line of convenient length is marked off and measured with great accuracy. Another point is chosen for the apex of the triangle, and the angles it makes from each end of the base-line are measured. From these angles and the base-line the area of the triangle is calculated. This process is continued until the whole piece of land is covered with a network of triangles.

A *theodolite* is used to measure these angles. This instrument is a telescope mounted on a tripod to bring it to eye-level, and fitted with micrometer microscopes.

The surveyor now has two new scientific instruments for making accurate measurements. One is the *geodimeter* which measures distance by recording the time taken for a beam of light sent from one point to be reflected back to it from another point miles away. As the speed of light is known, the distance can be calculated.

The second instrument is the *tellurometer*. It measures distance in the same way as the geodimeter but it uses radio waves instead of light.

A theodolite and a net work of triangulations

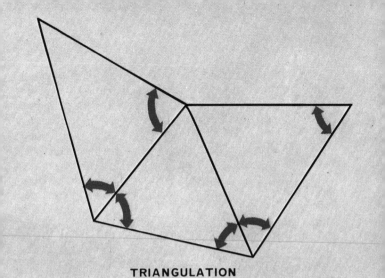

TRIANGULATION

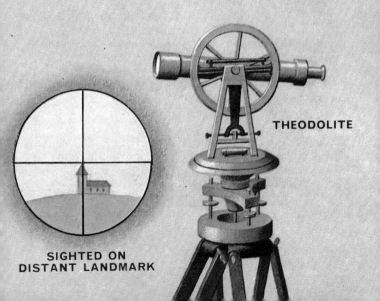

THEODOLITE

**SIGHTED ON
DISTANT LANDMARK**

Map-Making

You can experiment with the principles of map-making without the use of scientific instruments. All you need are a protractor, pencil, paper, a few drawing pins and a drawing board or piece of plywood for your paper.

Decide on a place to be mapped. A corner of the park is a good area, as it will have some suitable landmarks from which to take your bearings. Choose a good viewpoint and measure out your base-line. For a small area, a base-line of 500 paces should be sufficient. Place some stones or sticks to mark each end of the base-line, and start work at one end—which we will call 'A'.

Place your board and paper on a firm, level surface, and fasten your protractor to the paper with a pin through the central angle point. Make sure that the straight bottom edge lies along the line of your base-line. Kneel down, and from immediately behind the centre pin, sight a landmark. Move another pin round the edge of the protractor until it is in line with the landmark, and press it into the paper. You now have your first angle reading which you can write down as in the following example:

	Angle from 'A'	Angle from 'B'
To Church Steeple	40°	
To Coppice		
To Tower		

When you have completed your readings at 'A', move your board to 'B' and take readings for the same landmarks, entering the details on your paper. You will then have two readings for each point.

Make a rough sketch of the area as a future helpful guide, marking in lake, paths, etc. (*Continued on page 50*).

Making a map

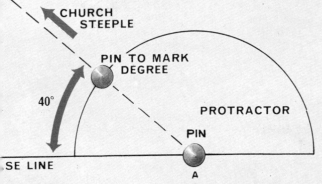

CHURCH STEEPLE

PIN TO MARK DEGREE

40°

PROTRACTOR

PIN

SE LINE

A

Map-Making (*Continued*)

The rest of the work on your map can be done at home.

On a sheet of paper, draw a line 50 mm long to represent the base line. Start at 'A' and carefully draw the lines from this point according to the angles you recorded. Then move your protractor along to 'B' and draw in the lines from that point. If you have matched the pairs of lines accurately, you will find that each landmark has been fixed at a point where its pair of lines meet.

From your knowledge of the area chosen, and from your rough sketch, you can now begin to draw in the details at the fixed points on your paper. When the area is fully mapped, rub out all the lines and triangles as these are no longer necessary.

Inside the back cover of this book is shown the sort of quick, rough sketch map you can draw if you are ever asked to direct anyone to a certain point in the area in which you live. This map not only gives road directions clearly from the station to Cedar Lodge (the destination), but also marks the more important landmarks to act as further guides. Details like these help to give assurance that the correct route is being followed.

Completing your map

COPPICE
TOWER
CHURCH
LAKE
BRIDGE
PARK
GATES
B   BASELINE   A

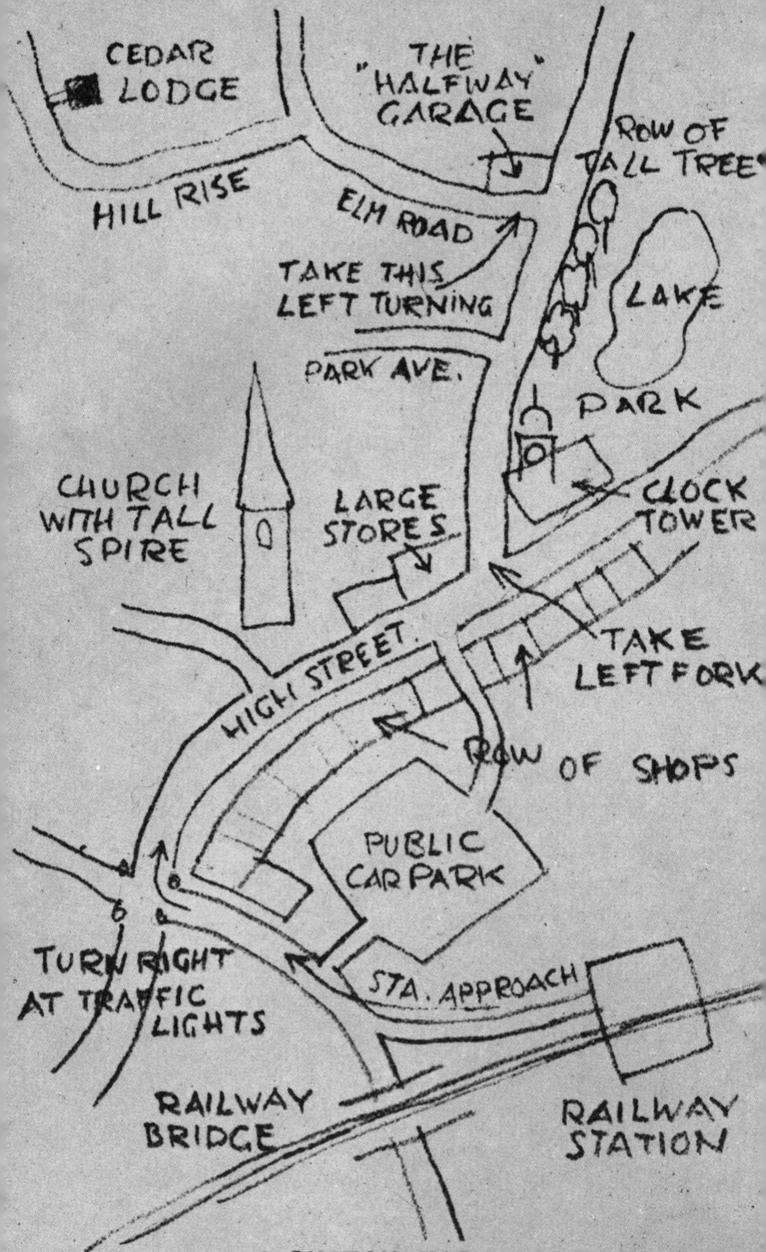

CEDAR LODGE

"THE 'HALFWAY' GARAGE"

ROW OF TALL TREES

HILL RISE

ELM ROAD

TAKE THIS LEFT TURNING

PARK AVE.

LAKE

PARK

CHURCH WITH TALL SPIRE

LARGE STORES

CLOCK TOWER

HIGH STREET

TAKE LEFT FORK

ROW OF SHOPS

PUBLIC CAR PARK

TURN RIGHT AT TRAFFIC LIGHTS

STA. APPROACH

RAILWAY BRIDGE

RAILWAY STATION

A SKETCH MAP